HAPPILY EVER CRAFTER

ONCE UPON AN ANIMAL CRAFT

ANNALEES LIM

Lerner Publications ◆ Minneapolis

First American edition published in 2020 by Lerner Publishing Group, Inc.

First published in Great Britain in 2018 by Wayland
Copyright © Hodder and Stoughton, 2018
All rights reserved.

Senior Commissioning Editor: Melanie Palmer
Design: Square and Circus
Illustrations: Supriya Sahai

Additional illustrations: Freepik

Lerner Publications Company
A division of Lerner Publishing Group, Inc.
241 First Avenue North
Minneapolis, MN 55401 USA

For reading levels and more information, look up this title at www.lernerbooks.com.

Main body text set in Billy Infant Regular 17/24.
Typeface provided by SparkyType.

Library of Congress Cataloging-in-Publication Data

Names: Lim, Annalees, author. | Sahai, Supriya, 1977– illustrator.
Title: Once upon an animal craft / Annalees Lim, Supriya Sahai.
Description: Minneapolis : Lerner Publications, [2019] | Series: Happily ever crafter | Audience: Age 7–11. | Audience: Grade 4 to 6. | "First published in Great Britain in 2018 by Wayland."
Identifiers: LCCN 2018050612 (print) | LCCN 2018053627 (ebook) | ISBN 9781541561991 (eb pdf) | ISBN 9781541558823 (lb : alk. paper)
Subjects: LCSH: Handicraft—Juvenile literature. | Animals in art—Juvenile literature.
Classification: LCC TT160 (ebook) | LCC TT160 .L48527 2019 (print) | DDC 745.5—dc23

LC record available at https://lccn.loc.gov/2018050612

Manufactured in the United States of America
1-46279-46263-11/27/2018

SAFETY INFORMATION:
Please ask an adult for help with any activities that could be tricky or involve cooking or handling glass. Ask adult permission when appropriate.

CONTENTS

ANiMaL KiNGDOM

The animal kingdom is vast—you will find animals in every country and ocean on the planet. They can be divided into different types such as mammals, birds, fish, reptiles, and insects and then divided again into vertebrates and invertebrates.

A vertebrate is any animal that has a backbone. There are thousands of different species of vertebrates, including birds, mammals, and some fish.

Invertebrates are animals that don't have a backbone. But many have skeleton-like armor on the outside of their body. This includes insects, snails, and lots of things that live under the sea. There are over a million different species of invertebrates, and there are still more being discovered.

FACT!
The most famous extinct animal is the dodo. Although it died out around the 17th century, it still remains a symbol of what happens when we don't look after the planet's animals.

Zoologists study animals to find out about how they live, what they eat, and which types of environments they thrive in. This book is perfect for any animal lover. You will find out lots of fun facts about many different kinds of animals, and you'll get to make some great crafts too. There are even fun ideas about how to plan a really wild party that will end up being a roaring success!

TOP TIP

There is a list of over 700 endangered animals who are close to being extinct, including sea turtles, tigers, and gorillas. You can do your part to help save these animals in many different ways. You can support charities and conservation projects or just try to make these craft activities as environmentally friendly as possible. By recycling any plastic, paper, or other materials you have at home and turning them into wonderful crafts, you will be helping the environment too.

CUTE CREATURE COSTUMES

These four costume projects are perfect if you have a party to go to, if you're starring in an animal-themed show, or if you just love dressing up! Collect materials from around your house—upcycle them, reuse them, and turn them into fantastically wild costumes.

RHINOCEROS

There are five species of rhino that live in the wild in Asia and Africa. These large, heavy animals love to eat plants. They have thick skin that is really sensitive. They cover it in mud to help prevent insect bites and sunburn.

You Will Need:

- GRAY PAINT (ACRYLIC IS BEST)
- PAINTBRUSH • OLD BASEBALL CAP
- LIGHT AND DARK GRAY FABRIC
- PAPER • SCISSORS • FABRIC GLUE
- PERMANENT MARKER

1. Paint an old baseball cap gray using paint. Leave it to dry.

2. Cut out two small ear shapes from some light gray fabric and two larger ear shapes from some darker gray fabric. You can paint any scrap fabric you have if you do not have the right color.

3. Cut out a small half circle shape from some white paper and roll it into a cone.

4. Stick the ears and cone onto the hat with the fabric glue.

5. Use a permanent marker to draw on eyes and a mouth.

COMPLETE THE COSTUME!

Wear all gray and attach a small fabric tail to the back of your top with a safety pin.

ELEPHANT

The African and Asian elephant might look similar, but you can tell the difference by their ears. The African elephant has large, wide ears that are a similar shape to the continent the animals come from, whereas the Asian elephant has smaller ears that are more rounded at the top. Which species will you choose to make?

You Will Need:

- 2 LARGE CEREAL BOXES • SCISSORS
- GRAY PAINT • PAINTBRUSH • WHITE CRAFT GLUE • PAPER • BLACK MARKER

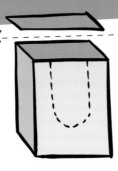

1. Cut the top off the cereal box and cut a "U" shape out of the front.

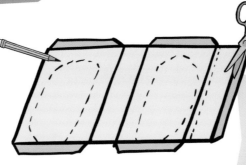

2. Cut two ears out from the front and back of another cereal box.

3. Use the side of the cereal box to make the trunk.

Fact

Elephants can suck up to 3½ gallons of water into their trunk. They will use it to drink or blow onto themselves to cool down.

4. Glue the ears and trunk to the first cereal box and paint it all gray.

5. Stick on two eyes and tusks made from white paper to the top of the box.

Where does an elephant pack its clothes when it goes on vacation?

In its trunk!

OCTOPUS

You Will Need:

- OLD T-SHIRT AND PANTS • 4 PAIRS OF LONG SOCKS • SCISSORS • NEWSPAPER • PERMANENT MARKERS • PAPER • WHITE CRAFT GLUE

There are about 300 different species of octopus. Did you know that they have beaks and three hearts? The name has the word "octo" (which means eight) because of the number of arms each octopus has. People often mistakenly call the arms tentacles.

1. Draw a head and eyes onto the T-shirt using the markers.

2. Cut off the waistband from some old pants (you can use the rest of the material for other craft projects).

3. Stuff the old long socks with scrunched-up pieces of newspaper, leaving 10 inches at the top. You will need eight of these "arms" in total.

4. Glue some small paper circles to the bottom of the arms to make the suckers.

FACT!
The word *animal* comes from the Latin word *animalis*, which means "living being."

5. Cut a slit at the top of the arms and use the two sections to tie each one onto the waistband. Space them evenly around the band.

BLUE WHALE

Blue whales are the largest living animals on the planet and can grow up to 100 feet—that's as long as two buses put together. They have hearts the size of a small car! Their mouths are so large that they can hold 100 tons of food and water, but their preferred food is krill. Krill are small, shrimp-like animals that are only a couple inches long, so blue whales will eat about 40 million of them a day!

You Will Need:

- LARGE CARDBOARD BOX • SCISSORS
- BLUE PAINT • PAINTBRUSH • FABRIC
- STAPLER • TAPE • MARKERS

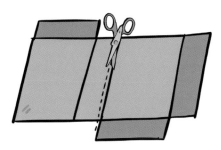

1. Flatten out a cardboard box and cut it in half.

2. Draw and cut out two whale body shapes and paint them blue. Once dry, tape the two whale shapes together at each end.

3. Draw on details, including the eyes, blowhole, and belly.

4. Bend the cardboard so that it is shaped like a body. Staple two strips of fabric to each shape. Make sure they are long enough to fit over your shoulders.

PARTY ANIMAL

Planning a great party doesn't have to be a chore, and it won't take you long to get organized if you follow these simple tips. If you can't take a trip to the zoo, make the zoo come to you. With these craft projects, recipes, and games, everyone will be sure to have a really wild time!

PERFECT PLANNING

It may seem like there are a million things to do to get ready for your party, but if you break it down by writing a list of all the important things, you'll soon be ready for the big day. Keep a list of what needs to be done so nothing gets forgotten. You'll need to think about these things:

HABITATS: A habitat is an animal's home. You can also create the perfect environment for your friends. Use the projects on page 16 to transform your party space into a family-friendly zoo.

CREATURE CREATIONS: There are so many different species in the animal kingdom that you could spend years making them all. Turn to page 28 to find four projects to start you off. Use them as extra decorations for your zoo or give them out as prizes to the winners of the games you play.

FEEDING TIME: Make sure you have plenty of snacks ready to feed your hungry herd! Follow the recipes on page 20 to make tasty treats, all with an animal theme.

MONKEYING AROUND: Parties are not complete without playing a few games. There are lots of fun ideas on page 12 for you to play, and they are fun to make too.

ZOO CREW!

Use this template to make this zoo-style invitation. Remember to include all the key information so that your guests have all they need to know to get to your party.

To:
Write the name of your zookeeper friend here.

What:
Say who is celebrating and why!

YOU ARE INVITED...

To: _____

What: _____

When: _____
_____

Dress code: _____

RSVP: _____

When and Where:
Include the date, time, and address of the party.

Dress code:
Say if you want people to turn up in special clothing.

RSVP:
Ask people to let you know if they can come.

PARTY GAMES

If you don't want your guests to run wild at your party, these games will help keep everyone entertained. Each game is simple to play and easy to make. You can get your guests to help too.

CHEATING CHEETAHS

A cheetah is a spotted animal that is part of the cat family. It is the fastest animal that lives on land, making it one of the world's most dangerous predators. A cheetah uses its long tail to help it steer and keep its balance as it runs.

You Will Need:
- CARDSTOCK OR THIN CARDBOARD
- WRAPPING PAPER • PAPER
- SCISSORS • GLUE STICK
- COLORED MARKERS

1. Cover one side of the cardstock with old wrapping paper and the other with regular paper. Repeat three more times so that you have four sheets.

2. Cut up each sheet into ten small cards. You will need forty cards to play.

3. Draw a zebra pattern on five cards.

4. Make seven more sets of five cards—cheetah spots, peacock feathers, giraffe markings, fish scales, panda patterns, tiger stripes, and crocodile skin.

HOW TO PLAY

Each player starts with four cards with the rest stacked in the middle. When it's your turn you can lay one to four cards down. They must be matching for you to put them down—or you can choose to lie. Tell the group what they are but keep them face down so no one can see them. If people think you're lying they can shout "Cheating Cheetah!" If you were lying, you have to pick up all the cards. If you were telling the truth, the person who shouted picks them up. If you don't want to risk lying, pick up one card from the stack. The first player to put down all their cards wins.

CHEEKY MONKEYS

Most monkeys, like humans, eat both plants and animals. They like to live on the ground and up high in tall trees. They are often confused with apes, but you can tell it's a monkey by checking if it has a tail. Tails help them to balance and hold onto the trees.

You Will Need:
- PAPER PLATES
- YELLOW PAINT
- BROWN MARKER
- SCISSORS
- PAINTBRUSH

1. Paint five plates yellow and leave to dry.

2. Cut out banana shapes from the edge of the plates. You should get three from each plate.

3. Use the brown marker to add markings and a stalk.

HOW TO PLAY

This is a race to see who can collect the most bananas in the fastest time. Hang the bananas on a clothes line. Make a starting line. Work in pairs to collect the most bananas. When the timer starts, link arms with your partner and race to the clothes line. You can only use one hand each. One person takes off the clothespin and the other takes the banana. Collect the bananas in a pile at the starting line. The timer stops when there are no more bananas to collect.

FLAMINGO BALANCE

Flamingoes are tall, brightly-colored birds with long legs. They are born with gray or white feathers which slowly change color over time depending on what they have been eating. The colors can range from pink to red or orange. They can fly as well as swim but are often seen wading or standing on one leg in shallow waters.

You Will Need:
- PAPER • SCISSORS
- BLACK MARKER • HOLE PUNCH
- STRING, RIBBON, OR ELASTIC

3. Color the end of the beak black with a marker.

2. Draw a beak shape and cut it out.

4. Punch some holes in the corners of the beak.

1. Fold a piece of paper in half.

HOW TO PLAY

Everyone who wants to play wears a beak. Everyone stands on one leg at the same time and tries not to wobble. The last person still standing on one leg is the winner.

5. Thread some ribbon, string, or elastic through the holes.

PANDA POTS

Giant pandas are well known for their black and white fur and love for eating bamboo. Did you know that, unlike the rest of the bear family, they never hibernate? When the winter comes they just climb down to where it is warmer and continue to eat the bamboo that they love.

What is a cheetah's favorite thing to eat?

Fast food !

You Will Need:
- MARKERS • PLASTIC CUPS
- PAPER • WHITE CRAFT GLUE
- SCISSORS

1. Draw a panda shape onto some paper and cut it out.

2. Glue it around a cup. Leave to dry. Repeat so that you have made five pots.

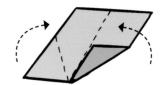

3. Fold pieces of paper like paper planes.

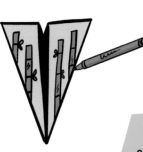

4. Draw a bamboo pattern onto the paper planes.

HOW TO PLAY

Spread the pots on the ground or on a table. Take turns throwing your colored bamboo planes into the pots. Whoever gets the most planes into the pots is the winner. Make it more challenging by moving the pots farther away or changing their height.

IN THE ZOO

Welcome your guests into a zoo that you've built full of wild animals. These projects are a great start, and you can add more to make your zoo bigger. Each animal needs a different space to live in. You could create dry deserts for the snakes and green jungles for the gorillas.

FEEDING TIME

Animals that live in zoos can't hunt for food in the same way they would in the wild. It's a zookeeper's job to know what each animal likes to eat and when. Fruit bats like fruit and seals love fish. Tigers eat meat that needs to be hidden first so they don't get lazy.

You Will Need:
- PLASTIC BOTTLE • TIN FOIL
- TAPE • CONSTRUCTION PAPER
- SCISSORS

1. Cut a clean plastic bottle in half and wrap the bottom in tin foil.

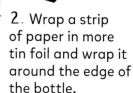

2. Wrap a strip of paper in more tin foil and wrap it around the edge of the bottle.

3. Make a handle from some more construction paper and tape it on.

4. Cut out letters to spell "feed" and stick them onto the front of the bucket.

TOP TIP
Use these buckets as serving dishes. Put sweet or savory snacks in them and display them together on your snack table.

BIRDS OF PARADISE

This group of exotic birds are usually found in the rainforests of Indonesia, Papua New Guinea, and Australia. Unlike most birds, they make nests on the ground. The males have very colorful feathers that they use to attract females. Some even do a dance!

You Will Need:
- SODA CANS • CONSTRUCTION PAPER OR MAGAZINES • TAPE • SCISSORS • GOOGLY EYES • (OPTIONAL: STRING)

1. Cover the lid and wrap the soda can in paper.

2. Stick a yellow paper circle onto the top of the can and cut a "V" shape into each side to make the beak.

3. Cut lots of feathers out from the different colored paper. Brightly-colored pictures in magazines are the best to use.

4. Make two paper feet from yellow paper.

5. Tape the feathers and feet to the can. Add googly eyes.

TOP TIP
Tie some string around the middle of the cans so that the birds can be hung up to look like they are flying.

POINT THE WAY

Signs are useful in zoos—they help you get to where you want to go. This craft will help you point your guests toward the food, tell them where the games are, or to just welcome people to your party.

You Will Need:
- CARDBOARD • BROWN PAINT
- PAINTBRUSH • PEN OR PENCIL
- BLACK MARKER • STRING

TOP TIP

Hang lots of signs together, pointing in different directions. Use a coat stand, door handles, or hang them from hooks.

1. Cut an arrow shape from some cardboard.

2. Paint the cardboard to look like wood with some brown paint.

3. Use a pencil or pen to make two holes at the top of the arrow.

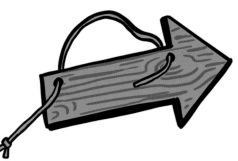

4. Thread some string through the holes and tie in place.

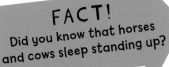

FACT!
Did you know that horses and cows sleep standing up?

5. Write your words onto the arrow using the black marker.

FUN
Food
GAMES

MAPS

Every zoo has a map to show where all the different animal enclosures are. Use this project to plan where your party zones will be, or use it as a wall decoration. During the party, people can draw their favorite animals on paper and tape them to the map. This is a great souvenir for you to keep at the end of the day.

You Will Need:
- LARGE SHEET OF PAPER • PAINT
- PAINTBRUSH • PAPER • SCISSORS
- MARKERS • TAPE • GLUE STICK

1. Cut out a large piece of paper. Flatten out cardboard boxes, packaging, or join smaller pieces of paper together with tape.

2. Paint the whole piece of paper in different shades of green and leave to dry.

3. Use yellow paint to draw wiggly lines all over the paper that will be the paths around your zoo.

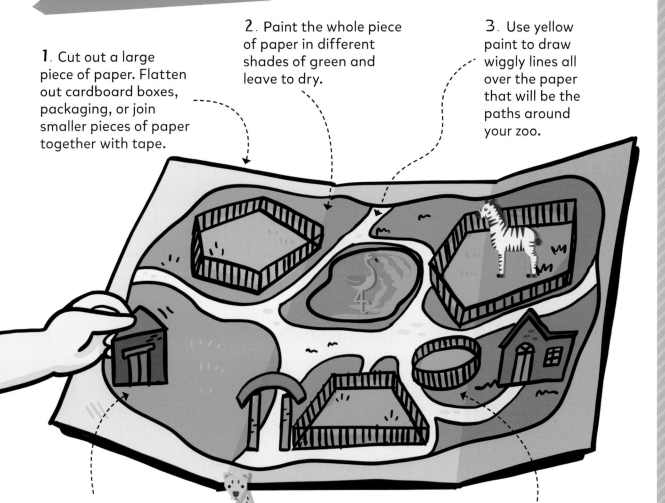

4. Draw small buildings on pieces of paper. Cut them out and glue them around the map. These could be gift shops or ticket offices.

5. Use markers to create enclosures that are ready for your animals to live inside.

TASTY TREATS

With these four delicious recipes that fit in perfectly with your animal-themed party, no one will be left feeling hungry. Remember to wash your hands before you start, and ask an adult to help you.

DOG BOWL BISCUITS

Dogs are a very popular domestic pet even though they are descended from wolves. They have a great sense of smell that is about 1,000 times better than ours, which is why you will find them often sniffing things out, especially delicious treats.

You Will Need:
- PAPER BOWL • CARDSTOCK
- SCISSORS • TAPE • PENCIL
- PAINT • PAINTBRUSH

1. Cut the bottom out of a paper bowl.

2. Make a cardstock circle that fits in the hole you've just cut out.

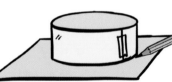

3. Draw around this circle onto some more cardstock to make the base.

4. Tape the parts together to make the dog bowl.

5. Paint the bowl a bright color, leaving a bone shape on the front.

6. Use icing pens to draw bone shapes onto your favorite cookies. Leave the icing to set before serving them in the dog bowl.

TROPICAL FISH PUNCH

Tropical water is warm and can be found around the equator. Here you will find tropical fish living in large groups called schools. There are thousands of different species. Most are very brightly colored, but they all have different patterns. People like to keep tropical fish as pets because they are pretty to look at. They have to live in special tanks with heaters so they don't get cold.

You Will Need:

- CLEAR PLASTIC CUPS • SAND
- WHITE CRAFT GLUE • TAPE
- GREEN PAPER OR PLASTIC BAGS
- PERMANENT MARKERS
- STRAWS • SCISSORS

1. Put some white craft glue on the bottom of the plastic cups and dip in sand.

2. Use permanent markers to decorate the cups with tropical fish.

3. Cut out leaf shapes from green paper or plastic bags.

4. Fix the leaves onto the top of straws with tape.

FRUIT PUNCH RECIPE

You can mix your favorite fruits and juices together to make any punch you like, or mix together the following for an ocean-like drink: Carefully crush blackberries in a bowl. Pour in some lemonade and ice cubes and stir well before serving in the cups.

CACTUS CAKES

The desert is a very dry, hot, and sandy environment that often gets very cold at night. This means only certain plants and animals live there. They all have their own special ways to keep cool and find water to survive.

1. Mix together some green icing and dip in the lady finger cookie. Leave to set.

2. Use the icing pen to add details to the cactus.

3. Use some buttercream frosting to cover the top of the cupcake.

4. Press the cactus into the cupcake.

5. Sprinkle some crushed cookies over the frosting and decorate with some gummy worms.

PENGUIN POPS

You Will Need:
- PLASTIC CUPS • CLING WRAP
- MILK CHOCOLATE • ICING PENS
- PUFFED RICE CEREAL
- POPSICLE STICKS

It's a common mistake to think that penguins live in the north pole and only like the freezing cold. Most penguins live in the southern half of the world, in countries such as South Africa, Australia, and Peru. They are good swimmers and dive to great depths, using their wings as flippers to help them move through the water to catch fish.

1. Line the plastic cups with some cling wrap.

2. Melt some milk chocolate into a bowl and mix in some cereal.

3. Spoon the mixture into the cups and press in the popsicle stick. Leave to set.

4. Remove the cups and peel off the cling wrap.

TO SERVE

Empty a bag of flour into a bowl and press it down firmly with the back of a spoon. Press the penguin pops into the flour so that it looks like they are gliding across the ice.

5. Decorate with icing pens to make the penguin. You will need eyes, a beak, wings, and feet.

CREATURE CRAFTS

Animal spotting is easy to do and can inspire fantastic crafts like these. Look around pet shops, go for a walk in the countryside, watch birds in a park, or even visit the zoo. Try out these projects and discover ways to adapt them yourself by making your favorite creatures from the animal kingdom.

UNDER THE SEA

You Will Need:
- CARDBOARD • SCISSORS
- PLASTIC BAGS • GLUE STICK
- CONSTRUCTION PAPER

Oceans are huge, and the deeper you go, the darker and colder it gets. There are lots of creatures that have learned to survive in deep water by collecting food that falls from above or by lighting up their bodies to help them see in the dark. It's a hard place for humans to explore, but more creatures are being discovered each time we dive.

1. Make two rectangular frames from cardboard.

2. Cut out wavy strips from plastic bags.

3. Stick these onto one of the frames, making sure they overlap slightly.

5. Cut out lots of fishy shapes and stick them onto the plastic.

4. Glue the other frame on top.

TOP TIP
Stick this onto the window so that the light shines through it and you can see the fish silhouettes swimming in the sunlight.

CAT CUSHION

Cats make great pets and are very playful creatures, although you will mostly find them napping. Did you know they sleep for about 16-18 hours a day? This cushion craft is a purr-fect present for any cat lover and great to cuddle up with when you're falling asleep.

You Will Need:
- OLD SWEATER • SCISSORS
- NEEDLE AND THREAD
- STUFFING AND CUSHION PAD
- (OPTIONAL: FABRIC GLUE)

1. Sew up the neck and the cuff of one sleeve.

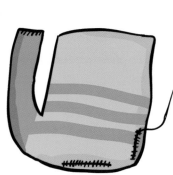

2. Tuck the other sleeve inside the body and sew up the hole.

3. First fill the sleeve with stuffing, then fill the body with a cushion pad. Sew up the bottom of the sweater.

4. Cut out a nose, eyes, whiskers, ears, and paws from scrap fabric or felt.

MEOW!

5. Glue or sew these onto the cushion.

Why are fish so smart?
Because they love to hang out in schools!

FARMYARD

You Will Need:
- LARGE PIECE OF CARDBOARD
- GREEN, RED, AND WHITE PAINT
- PAINTBRUSH • PAPER • SCISSORS
- TAPE • CARDSTOCK • GLUE STICK
- SMALL CARDBOARD BOX

Farmers grow plants and look after animals. They have lots of land that is surrounded by fences to keep the animals from getting lost. Grow your farm by making different fields that will sit next to this one and fill them with your favorite farmyard animals.

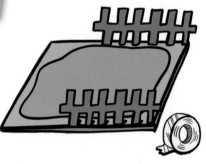

1. Paint a large sheet of cardboard green and let dry.

2. Fold a long strip of brown paper accordian-style into six equal parts. Draw a cross on the front, making sure it touches the sides.

3. Cut out the cross shape and open it up. Stick it around the edge of the green cardboard. Make enough to go around the whole edge.

4. Paint a small box red and white and leave to dry.

5. Fold a piece of dark cardstock in half and tape it on to make the roof. Cut some slits into the box to make the doors open.

6. Stick the barn in the field.

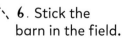

WISE OWL POTS

Owls come out at night and have large eyes to help them see things in the dark. Unlike most birds, they do not make their own nests. Instead, they prefer to hide in holes in trees or even use old nests that other birds have made and don't use anymore.

1. Draw a line around the middle of the plastic bottle with two triangles on top.

2. Cut this out carefully and cover the edges with tape so they are not sharp.

You Will Need:

- LARGE PLASTIC BOTTLE • SCISSORS
- TAPE • WHITE CRAFT GLUE
- CONSTRUCTION PAPER • BLACK MARKER

3. Cover with a layer of white craft glue and stick on torn bits of paper. Leave to dry.

4. Cut out some paper shapes for the eyes, wings, and beak.

IT'S A HOOT!

5. Glue the shapes onto the bottle base and cover the whole thing with another layer of white craft glue.

SOFT SHARK

There are hundreds of species of sharks. Some are as big as whales, while others are as small as your hand. There are no vegetarian sharks, but that does not mean that we are on the menu. Sharks have no interest in hurting us.

1. Draw a shark shape on a piece of paper and cut it out.

2. Use the paper shark as a template and cut out two more from some fabric.

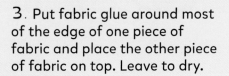

Why does a cow eat grass all day long?

Because it thinks it is a lawn moo-er!

3. Put fabric glue around most of the edge of one piece of fabric and place the other piece of fabric on top. Leave to dry.

4. Stuff the shark with scrap fabric until it is full and then glue the gap together.

5. Decorate with more scrap fabric to make fins, eyes, and teeth.

PORCUPINE PRINT

Porcupines are nocturnal animals, which means they like to be awake at night. They eat mainly plants, but they are prey for some larger animals. To protect themselves from predators they use thousands of sharp sticks on their backs, called quills, as armor.

You Will Need:
- BROWN AND WHITE PAINT • GLUE STICK • PAINTBRUSH • THICK PAPER • PAINT TRAY • SMALL TWIG • BLACK MARKER • GOOGLY EYE

2. Spread white and brown paint onto a paint tray.

3. Dip the twig into the paint and print it onto the back of the body. Leave to dry.

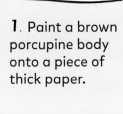

1. Paint a brown porcupine body onto a piece of thick paper.

4. Use a black marker to draw details, including the nose, mouth, arms, and legs.

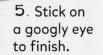

5. Stick on a googly eye to finish.

MEERKAT FINGER PAINTING

Meerkats are small mammals from Africa that live in large groups called clans or mobs. They are very protective of the many underground tunnels where they live and leave a scent to mark their territory. You might see them stand up on their back legs, looking out for predators while their other family members are busy looking for food.

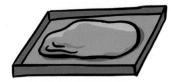

1. Mix up some light brown paint and spread it evenly on a paint tray.

2. Press your finger into the paint and make a print on a sheet of paper.

3. Use your thumb to make another print on top of the first. Leave to dry.

4. Cut out a tail, arms, feet, a nose, and ears from paper.

5. Glue the paper parts onto the fingerprints and draw on any smaller details like eyes or special markings.

30

SWIMMING SEA TURTLE

Most sea turtles have hard shells that protect their bodies. They swim long distances through the ocean and often face many dangers, one of which is pollution from plastic. They mistake the plastic for food and eat it by accident.

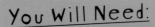

You Will Need:
- PLASTIC BOTTLE • SCISSORS
- TAPE • WHITE CRAFT GLUE
- CONSTRUCTION PAPER
- PAINTBRUSH • GREEN AND BLUE TISSUE PAPER

1. Cut off the bottom of the plastic bottle and cover the edges with a strip of tape.

2. Make a head and four fins from dark green paper and tape them onto the smaller plastic bottle.

3. Tear up small pieces of light green tissue paper and glue them onto the bottle using craft glue. Repeat with blue tissue paper onto the top part of the bottle. Leave to dry.

TOP TIP
This craft is great for reducing the amount of plastic waste you throw away!

4. Cover the edge of the top of the bottle with green paper to look like long seaweed.

5. Balance the turtle on top of the bottle's cap to make it look like it is swimming through the seaweed.

ANIMAL PUZZLE

CAN YOU FIND THE ANSWERS TO THESE QUESTIONS?

1. Which sloth has climbed the highest?

2. How many flowers can you count?

3. Where is the parrot hiding?

4. Which sloth is different?